M000023674

Book One

Spirituality for REAL

Beyond the Incense
and Meditation

WakunDaMa

© WakunDaMa 2019

Print ISBN: 978-1-73335-740-1
eBook ISBN: 978-1-73335-741-8

All rights reserved. This book or any portion thereof may not be reproduced or used in any manner whatsoever without the express written permission of the publisher except for the use of brief quotations in a book review.

Cover by Toelke Associates
Published by WakundaMa® Publishing
www.wakundama.com

CONTENTS

INTRODUCTION

A gentle and respectful hug to you. I missed you. It's so good to see you finally.

I love you, dear friend. I may not have met you yet physically, but the journey we will have traveled will in the end have been the same one. The road you travel will not be an easy one, but I want to connect with you wherever you are and reassure you that all is actually OK.

Rest assured. Despite your unique challenges, you are not alone. You are loved. You are important. You are of immeasurable worth and value. And it's not because of what you have achieved or done. It is because you exist.

You are beautiful. You are a perfect, radiant example of why there is life. I write this to remind you of this fact. I write this even more to help you rebelieve this fact.

Just the same, you will doubt me. In fact, at many times, I will doubt me! And so I would like to share just an aspect of my journey of doubt. I share it to let you know I'm really on the same road you are traveling.

But more than sharing a part of my personal journey, I want to share some practicalities regarding this road called life. I share with you for the reason that you have read as far as this sentence... you're longing for greater purpose and meaning.

This is the realm of belief, religion, and spirituality. To the parts of you that are skeptical of things spiritual, I welcome your skepticism, because it tells me you seek deeper meaning than what has been provided and will not settle for general explanations. To the parts of you that are already spiritual, I want to renew your sense of what it means to be spiritual.

In my writing, I want to share practices for finding courage in the face of great fear, purpose in the midst of hopelessness, and nurture in the middle of loneliness. I am grateful to be able to share with you.

– WakunDaMa

CHAPTER 1
Spirituality for Real

I magine achieving complete happiness in every aspect of your life. Someone interviews you and asks what is left for you to accomplish in life, what else are you planning to do? You answer, "Nothing. I'm happiest where I am at this moment."

Real-world spirituality is the ability to be happy despite what at times may feel like great hopelessness, loneliness, and unfairness. More important, it provides the reason to act humanely and generously even to those who may seem to act unkindly and selfishly towards you. Real-world spirituality is knowing that the day you cease to treat others with unconditional dignity and respect is the day that life becomes petty and purposeless.

There are an abundance of religions and new-age beliefs that already deliver spirituality to you. But most deliver spirituality in a way that is mysterious, sacred, and vague.

The dictionary describes a *mystic* as someone who believes in mysticism. It then describes *mysticism* as a belief that personal union with the Divine is based upon intuition, sudden insight, or vague, unsubstantiated thought about something. This definition conveys the mystic as someone who is vague and mysterious and whispers inside smoky, incense-filled rooms.

I like to see the mystic as one who utilizes insight, intuition, and guidance to shape his or her own reality into actual existence. That definition brings forth the mystic from passivity to healthy assertiveness.

Consider the mystic as one who manifests his or her reality into actual being.

When I state "manifesting your own reality," I am not talking about making up imaginary things in a fantasy world. I am talking about explicit actions you take to accept or reject opportunities in your life, but you often manage to blind yourself from recognizing this when you have done it. I am also talking about you being able to exude qualities that shape life around you, often to the surprise and amazement of yourself. As you become the mystic, you shall find and understand how the people, things, and events in the world actually cater to your needs.

When I describe real-world spirituality, I aim to demystify and bring a frankness and practicality to the idea of spirituality. For years I lived like many others trying to understand the spiritual as being mysterious, something that frankly didn't feel all that real. Many millions of people flock to places of worship in order to be socially acceptable or to cast their grievances before imaginary beings that float invisibly above the clouds; then they drop that spiritual devotion and continue with the same daily quest of amassing wealth and fighting enemies physically, socially, or economically. To many, spirituality is a separate psychological and imaginary place that provides comfort in a dangerous and unpredictable world. I now know and understand differently. The real spiritual world is this very world we are in, here and now, with everything to do with your purpose in life.

I once listened to Susan describe how she used to be a timid and dependent person needy of other people's support. Susan wondered why her relatives didn't want to see her. She would visit them, and would do things to cater to them, but they would not return the favor. Susan was miserable and felt as if something was wrong with her, or something was burdensome or unattractive about her, for people to avoid her. Then one day something shifted within her and she changed. If no one would come and see her, then "So what!" Instead of a soft exterior she had a no-nonsense and tough exterior. Susan would start taking care of herself, and if it upset loved ones, then that was their problem, not hers. No longer would her self-esteem depend upon others. She started loving and taking care of herself.

Then, oddly, her sister could not get enough of her. She became in great demand by all her relatives. She nurtured and strengthened her spirit, exuded newer qualities and energies, and changed her reality. She created her own reality by deciding what to believe from within first. A side effect of Susan changing herself was that everyone around her changed. In this regard, Susan was the mystic. This is an example of Spirituality…for Real.

So, as you now consider spirituality, ask yourself if your goal is to be comfortably mystified by life and continue to be at the mercy of arbitrary events. If you are comfortable in a routine of religious mystery, then continue to view spirituality as some hidden dimension such as heaven, purgatory, or hell. But know that limiting your spiritual existence to a hidden world separate from your everyday life will serve you only if your goal is to remain mystified.

However, if you would like to take ownership in shaping your life, then start taking regard of your spiritual existence. Please regard your existence on Earth as of greater purpose than a mere physical existence of one person. Please understand the concept that this spirit of you has always existed, is here in the present, and will always exist.

This view of an eternal spirit will help you in challenging times. This view of the eternal spirit will free you to live as the mystic rather than the mystified. You will no longer need to be the victim who complains how life would be better if only things in life treated you better. This view of spirit will empower you to change your world.

To find the real-world spirituality, don't bother waiting to go to heaven or hell, because the real spiritual world is here and now. While this physical existence on Earth isn't the whole picture, it is still very much part of the spiritual world. If you want to understand spirituality in tangible action, don't look to a temple, church, mosque or synagogue. Instead, look to everyday courageous acts in human life. Look to what allows simple, ordinary, human beings in the midst of the tragic aftermath of violence or natural disaster to do heroic things while acting with great humanity. Even look to the many unsung steps of courage that you have exercised up to now to have continued showing up and continued trying despite many things in life not seeming to go your way.

This journey you are living out from your birth up to now, with many more steps to travel, is your Spirituality for Real.

CHAPTER 2
Is Your Mind Spirituality?

Reading this book may seem to be mostly a mental exercise. And so, one might equate the mind with your spirituality. This view can take you quite far in shaping your life. Your mind can control your physical actions, what you speak, and how you behave. In a very direct physical way your mind can control matter. So, in a way you could conclude that the mystic is the result of attitude and thoughts of the mind. And so the mind can create without the need for spirituality—or maybe spirituality is the power of the mind.

In 1839, Edward Bulwer-Lytton wrote, "The pen is mightier than the sword." That was a reference to the fact that mere physical weapons of war pale in comparison to the human ideas that are behind their use. The idea and motivation that you implant in the minds of men have the power to determine the creation, use, and need of weapons to control reality. Today, when the most advanced technologies exist for military use, the power of "psychological warfare" (the mind) is taken very seriously. Properly broadcasted news coverage has the power to sway the public to save millions of starving people in one country or wage war upon millions of people in another.

I bring in the context of war because that is an activity that so many humans believe is real, undeniable, and inevitable. There is not one person that will doubt the mind's ability to cause war because we continually witness how thoughts and beliefs directly translate into acts of violence. Depending upon the perspective behind those thoughts the acts of violence get justified or berated. However, skepticism exists about the human mind's ability to cause the real and undeniable creation of life, happiness, peace, and love. Holding on to this skepticism will not serve you well.

All perspectives, philosophies, and beliefs are true, but not all of them will serve you well. You decide what to think will best serve you. Make conscious life choices to understand the purpose and need of spirituality in your life. Know that spirituality is always a part of your life, whether you like it or not.

> *Criticize not how a statement is wrong. Rather, seek to*
> *understand the how or why a statement becomes true.*
> – WakunDaMa

No matter what you think, you are spiritual. Do you believe that spirituality is part of your life? If you don't, then good, you are a skeptic and a seeker of truth. Please read on; this book is meant for you. If you do believe you are spiritual, this book is also meant for you.

Many of us have been taught that spirituality exists in the mind, but as you read further, I will challenge you to broaden your horizons and accept things outside your mind. I do not deny that all things can be viewed as forms of mental exercises, but doing so will limit you and not best serve you. You can use many more dimensions beyond just the mental and physical world if you are willing.

For example, if you are seeking to find love in this world, you could search for it by studying the chemical reactions in the brain. Some scientists say that feelings of love are the result of chemical reactions involving endorphins, pheromones, and neurotransmitters. If you believe that scientific fact, inevitably you will find it to be so, but I still think many of us would dispute whether love can ever be understood scientifically. If your goal is to find love, you could stay within the mind and try to master love through scientific thinking and chemical reactions. However, this is not likely to work well.

Imagine you are in a room with one glass window to see outside. This window is also the only source of light to the room. Now imagine covering this window with black paint to block the light. It is dark. You can see nothing.

Now let's scrape off some paint. Just a coin-sized opening, so that some light comes through. Light comes through, providing just a little light in an otherwise dark room. If you look through this small opening, you can see the outside again. You can see everything through this small opening and almost as well as when the window was completely uncovered. However, with the smaller opening you must strain and tilt your head to see everything outside.

Scrape off another spot of paint on a different part of the window. You will have the same results, but notice that some things on the outside are a little easier to see than with the first opening you created and some are harder to see. Scrape off another spot of paint on that window and look through it. Do it again. As you peek through the different openings, you will see the outside through slightly different perspectives. The total of all those slightly different perspectives will be greater than any one perspective.

Looking at life through just the mind is like looking at the world through one small opening. As you scrape off more openings, you get other perspectives and start to gain new insights. This book is about scraping off the paint that is covering your view of life. As you read on, we will scrape off more of the paint, continually improving the quality of your view. Let us begin by making our first scrape to look at the power of mind over matter.

Mind Over Matter: Speed

A classic example of the mind's ability to shape reality was the quest to run one mile in under four minutes. One mile is about four laps around a standard 400-meter track. While many athletes can easily do the first three laps in three minutes, the ability to keep up the pace for the final lap seemed to remain challenging. In 1936, a man by the name of Jack Lovelock held the world record in the mile, and he wrote, "Running three minutes for three laps is becoming too easy." However, no one—not even Jack Lovelock—was capable of keeping this so-called easy pace for one more lap. Jack could accomplish 75% of a mile easily and found the final 25% much more difficult. Jack Lovelock never succeeded in running the mile in four minutes or less.

If you could achieve 75% of your goal easily, surely you could achieve the last lap with just a little more effort. Back in 1936, the human body would break down during the final 25% of a mile. Experienced distance runners knew that how fresh you felt after the first three laps didn't mean much and it would be wise to conserve energy for the fourth and final lap. For years, many runners would come close to the four-minute barrier, but never attain it. The power of the human mind was so strong it became accepted that no human could run one mile in less than four minutes. It became a law of nature.

Scientists used to think the sound barrier was impossible to break, until it was broken in 1947. In 1947 the barrier to the four-minute mile still held. In 1953, a runner named John Landy came close. He ran one mile in four minutes and two seconds, but somehow, no matter how hard he tried, cutting out those last two seconds seemed impossible for him.

In 1953, a handful of men set out on attempts to break the four-minute barrier. On May 6, 1954, Roger Barrister finally did it. During the race, when Roger reached the third lap in slightly over three minutes he commented, "the effort was imperceptible." In fact, he had two other undistinguished runners run with him throughout the entire mile, to help pace him. All of them could have stopped at the third lap and finished in three minutes or less, feeling fresh. What happened during the fourth and final lap was quite different. Roger Barrister described his fourth lap of his world-record run as follows:

> The world seemed to stand still, or did not exist. The only reality was the next two hundred yards of track under my feet…

> My body had long since exhausted all its energy, but it went on running just the same. The physical overdraft came only from greater willpower. This was the crucial moment when my legs were strong enough to carry me over the last few yards, as they could never have done in previous years…I leapt at the tape like a man taking his last spring to save himself from the chasm that threatens to engulf him.

> My effort was over and I collapsed almost unconscious, with an arm on either side of me. It was only then that real pain overtook me. I felt like an exploded flashlight with no will to live; I just went on existing in the most passive physical state without being quite unconscious. Blood surged from my muscles and seemed to fell me. It was as if all my limbs were caught in an ever-tightening vice. I knew that I had done it before I even heard the time.

> – Roger Barrister, *The First Four Minutes*

Roger Barrister broke the four-minute barrier by 0.6 seconds, setting the new world record, by having his mind allow his body to be pushed beyond what his mind would normally consider an acceptable level of fatigue. Only after crossing the finish line and stopping did his mind allow him to experience the full brunt of the pain that he would have normally experienced before the finish line.

The unwritten law that humans can't run faster than a four-minute mile was no more. Once Roger Barrister proved the impossible was possible, it only took 46 more days for runner John Landy to best Roger Barrister's time by 1.5 seconds. Runners have continued to whittle further past the four-minute mile barrier. Today, the world record pace is more than 16 seconds better than Roger Barrister's time.

Mind Over Matter: Strength

In the 1940s, a man named Moshe Feldenkrais found that many of the causes of physical pain or disorder lay entirely in the mind. He started his career as a nuclear physicist working alongside Nobel Laureate physicist Marie Curie. Moshe was also an avid soccer player until he suffered a knee injury. Insistent on avoiding knee surgery, he set out on a path to regain his movement without physically repairing his knees. He regained full mobility of his legs without doing anything to directly fix his knees. It was said that X-rays of his knees still showed debilitating damage, which should have prevented him from walking without great pain and effort, yet Moshe was walking with no pain and little effort. Whereas conventional medicine was focused on fixing things to allow you to best walk the way you used to walk, Moshe figured out how to make subtle changes in his style of walking that did not require repairing his knees. He had mastered the art of human movement. Moshe's findings formed the physical therapy known today as the Feldenkrais Method®. NBA hall of fame player, Julius Erving, known for acrobatic aerial maneuvers, was reportedly Moshe's client.

In Feldenkrais, the goal is to cure chronic muscle tension, pain, weakness, and fatigue by educating the motor-neuron-controlling parts of the brain. Rather than using surgery or medication to change muscle behavior, more subtle techniques of self-discovery of one's ability to precisely control movement could lead to better posture, the elimination of back pain, and better athletic performance. Moshe found three reasons for muscles getting tired:

1. The neurons in the brain controlling the muscles stop exciting the muscle,

2. The nerve endings connected to the muscle tissue begin exhausting their supply of chemicals and get too much waste, or

3. The muscle cells genuinely fatigue by burning up all their fuel and getting too much lactic acid.

Moshe found that when a muscle is repeatedly used until it gets weak, it still is actually very strong. If an electric pulse is sent directly through the nerve that feeds the supposedly tired muscle, the muscle will once again contract without any fatigue. The fatigue is not in the muscle itself, but in the brain, which is responsible for sending fewer electric pulses. When the brain reduces the electric pulses sent through the nerves driving the leg muscles, the muscles feel as if fatigued and contract with less strength.

Moshe observed that a great deal of what causes a human muscle to fatigue and weaken is the brain. He found that if the brain could somehow be convinced to stop creating a tired muscle sensation, the muscles would once again contract strongly.

The brain, if never able to reduce its electrical pulses to the nerves, would eventually cause the nerve endings to fatigue, preventing the pulses from reaching the muscles. Again, the experience would feel like muscle fatigue. However, Moshe found that even when the nerve endings fatigued, the actual muscles would still be strong. If both the brain and nerve endings were fatigued but somehow electric pulses were sent directly to the muscle, the muscle would again continue to contract with great strength.

Eventually, the actual muscle cells deplete themselves of fuel, get laden with lactic acid, and actually fatigue when electric pulses are directly sent. This would be genuine muscle fatigue, something humans rarely, if ever, encounter.

When a runner feels his muscles getting tired, most likely his muscles are still at full strength and it his mind that has shut down his strength. Ultimately, human muscular strength potential is much greater than we would believe. When someone's muscles fatigue, it's mostly just the brain.

The soreness and pain that can be associated with muscle tiredness comes from the brain, without which there would be no such sensation. Physical pain is known to be a nerve-to-brain event. Painkillers work by interfering with the transmission of signals in the brain or nerves. Pain feels so real, yet is merely in the mind. It is becoming ever more clear in modern medicine that the mind is so much more than subtle abstract thoughts; it is a very large factor behind actual human physical strength.

Mind Over Matter: Health

If a person is fooled into thinking that a sugar pill is actually a drug, it tends to have the effect of assisting that person as if it were true. This is known as the *placebo effect*, and modern medicine recognizes it as real. However, modern medicine considers it a psychological effect that works because it puts the person in a positive frame of mind, which then allows the body to perform its best in healing itself.

Few will deny that an ill person with strong inner and external emotional support will recover more effectively than if under great emotional stress and lacking emotional support. Physiologically, the brain is known to emit chemicals to increase strength, cause relaxation, enhance deep thought, and control pain. The psychological state a brain goes through will impact the performance of the physical body. Western medicine considers good mental state as something that enhances core treatments such as surgery, medications, or physical therapy. There is little credibility in the idea that one's state of mind could actually become the primary healer and that treatments such as surgery, medications, or physical therapy might actually be only a secondary means of healing. You can continue to think that the psychological state is merely a secondary healer, but it will not best serve you. If you think this way, you will cause it to be so, and you will not get the full benefits of healing through the mind.

Earlier I described scraping out a small peephole in a window covered with black paint. Don't restrict your view to just one small peephole. You can continue to restrict your views this way, and everything will continue to work just like you expect it to occur, with all its "normal" surprises and disappointments. Challenge yourself to scrape off more of the paint off the window.

Will you dare think differently?

Try thinking the opposite of what you normally think. Consider that your mind can become the core treatment, and that it is the surgery, medications, and physical therapy that are necessary enhancements of the psychology. Consider that your psychological state is the primary cause of your health and that physical activities merely help your primary cause. If you dare to think the opposite, you will scrape off more paint. You will have a greater view and perspective of reality. You will have more options and choices. This will serve you well.

The placebo effect acknowledges that some things in the real world are influenced by what you think. Ironically, even if a placebo pill has helped people, science will still declare this as not real. That is to say if it works for you but no scientific basis backs it up, it is not real. Science considers the healing ability of most herbs, vitamins, and supplements as placebo. The typical belief is that the placebo effect is merely an auxiliary emotional thing, but not the primary thing.

So why not consider the placebo effect?

Consider taking a chance on accepting what you cannot explain. You have complete freedom to think or not think whatever you would like, but once you make your choice, ask yourself, "Will this choice serve me well?"

CHAPTER 3
Holistic Health

H ealth is traditionally thought of as the result of physical well-being. It is also a byproduct of emotional well-being, which is often impacted by one's mental well-being. When one is in a comfortable and healthy state of being, then spirituality is merely a mental exercise, where in the ideal state, one can make thoughts conquer matter. Here spirituality is not very impactful and not very important.

But when your health begins to falter and you seem to lack the ability to heal yourself, only then are you challenged to consider asking why this is happening...or why must life be plagued with "bad events." When things you wish to be able to take for granted fall apart, the opening for spirituality for real enters. And it's not as if you or most of us very much like having this opening for the spiritual; I mean in a way it is so much more comfortable and easy if life followed a simple rule that if you behave well you are always rewarded with good and always spared hurt or harm—including being spared death.

Death and illness are inevitabilities of the human state. And no amount of mind control will ever be able to stop illness, aging, and inevitable death. It's the way it is supposed to be. And yes, there's a part of all of us that as we accept implications of our mortality, we say to ourselves, "This sucks!" And when we willingly acknowledge that area that says "This sucks!" we enter into real-world spirituality. And so our health and our mortality are very much undeniable true entrances into deepening spirituality.

Health as Mind and Body

As a child I was plagued by a multitude of food and environmental allergies and asthma, as well as chicken pox, flu, and colds. I remember getting many kinds of injections. A room vaporizer, taking antibiotics, aspirin, and cough syrup was an everyday part of my life.

My father encouraged me not to take medication, to allow my body to develop its own "medicine." That was my first introduction to the idea that the body can cure itself. Being sick from the flu several times a year was normal for me. By the time I got to high school, I decided I had had enough of being sick, and so one night when I felt the onset of the flu, I wrapped myself in layers of clothing, put on a few blankets, and managed to sweat my flu away by the next morning. I started listening to recorded meditations designed to improve my memory to do better in school. I was intrigued by the physical effects of the meditation and how it allowed me to combat illness. The next time I felt the onset of the flu, I wrapped myself extremely warmly, used the meditation, and recovered completely by midday. The next time I felt the flu, I meditated, visualizing intense white-hot light shining down upon me and burning the flu away. I recovered within an hour.

A shift occurred and no longer did I experience multiple flu's a year. It would take another twenty years before I would succumb to the flu again. I can still get the flu, but I find it infrequent. I may still cough and sneeze, but I'll recover quickly. I'll sometimes take cough lozenges or aspirin to lessen symptoms and help my body's own natural healing ability. In the end, I know that the larger part of my healing will come from within me.

I understand few medications can counter a flu virus. Most medications counter secondary bacterial infections that might occur, help suppress symptoms that interfere with your body healing itself, or train your immune system to recognize and counter particular strains of a virus. Modern Western medicine has gone a long way towards the magic pill that will instantly cure anything. That is still a dream, and the only thing that is instant is symptom suppression. The long-term health ultimately depends upon what our bodies can achieve and the healing choices we make in addition to any medicine we decide to take. This view is sometimes called *integrative medicine* or *holistic wellness.*

Modern Western medicine views well-being as made up of two parts: good physical health and good mental health. Physicians and specialists prescribe drugs and perform surgery to counteract physical ailments, whereas psychiatrists and psychologists use drugs and/or talk therapy to manage harmful thoughts and emotions. Western medicine acknowledges that attitude and faith can influence the success of recovery from an ailment; however, attitude and faith are considered conditions of the mind.

By this view, attitude and faith, things of the mind, are not considered a primary source of healing. At best, these only help reduce any harmful emotional stress, but even that is largely thought of as electrochemical processes that can be controlled effectively with drugs. In this traditional view, concepts of spirituality or religion merely exist in the mind and are therefore ultimately traceable to electrochemical processes.

Do you believe your spirituality is merely chemistry?

Western medicine emphasizes objective analysis of the symptoms uninfluenced by emotions. Understanding the illness is emphasized more than the person. Ideally, for the same illness, it should not matter who the person being treated is. In classic *allopathic* (Western) medicine you're more likely to be thought of as one patient among a thousand rather than a person with unique qualities and needs.

Despite our acceptance of these Western medicine ideas, many of us practice a third part to well-being by asking, What about acknowledging the actual health of the personality? What about the spirit and sense of purpose of the person? Religious leaders, psychotherapists, and your friends and family touch on this area. This is the arena that holistic wellness tries to bring into the picture.

Mind, Body, and Spirit

More of us have come to understand medicine is about healing the total person. The philosophy is not to react to symptoms, but to resolve the cause of the illness. This is holistic medicine. A healthy person is viewed as a balance of mental, physical, and spiritual well-being. Although spiritual health is now being embraced, it is still considered secondary to mental or physical solutions. Spiritual healing is considered a religious issue. As I'll describe later, spirituality and religion are different.

Holistic Wellness - Healing the Total Person

Body
Exercise, yoga, Physician, medication, diet, herbs, acupuncture.

Mind
Psychotherapy, medication, rest, meditation, vacation.

Spirit
Religion, pastor, master, yoga, meditation, acupuncture, vacation.

Achieve health and quality of life by a balance of the three modalities of mind, body, and spirit.

For those of you interested in a balanced, holistic approach to health, the above pie chart illustrates widely accepted approaches to being a balanced, healthy person. Many of these are considered "alternative" medical therapies. Most don't cleanly address just mind, body, or spirit. Usually each therapy overlaps in all three. The differences are that some modalities (mode or method of treatment) may be emphasized more than others. Spirit and mind are sometimes considered the same thing. The concept of a spirit is a mental thing, and therefore it's part of the mind. When we talk about mind, body, and spirit, most of us are still talking about mind and body, with spirit being considered an idea within the mind.

Most tend to treat body and mind as the primary and secondary aspects of life, leaving the spirit as the third or even fourth aspect of human life. We may believe the spirit is good to have, but by no means a necessity. If that is the model of life you choose, it may function OK. The only problem with that model is that it's the choice to be passive at the mercy of hope and chance. It's about having no choice and very little power. In contrast, the model of understanding that spirit is the reason and purpose for life is a path toward choice and empowerment. You will reshape your world and have ownership and understanding of how you have reshaped your world.

Even if you decide not to make a choice, you are still making a choice that will reshape your world, only it may be reshaped in a way you may not wish for. But you will have done so because it's what you're used to and comfortable with. You will "allow the shaping of your world for you," and have a sense of little ownership or understanding of how your world is. The benefit of making no choice is the privilege of blaming others for what you don't like about where you are.

Let's make the choice to bring clarity to the phrases "Mind, Body, and Spirit," "Mind, Body, and Soul," and "Body and Soul". These phrases are OK for some purposes, but I have found it makes more sense to look at things as Physical, Mental, or Energetic. In this context acupuncture tends to fall in the energetic modality.

- **Physical Modalities**: Traditional treatments such as mending a broken bone with a cast or surgery to clear a constricted artery are physical because they can be touched and seen.

- **Mental Modalities**: Psychotherapy, psychiatry, and meditation. These are considered thoughts that have a direct impact on how you behave or act.

- **Energetic Modalities**: Nuclear physics states that matter is made of energy. And so human bodies, being matter, are also composed of energy. We call this energy behind our living matter "Life Energy" or "Bioenergy."

Preceding any physical ailment is an irregularity or blockage in our bioenergy. This is the principle behind acupuncture. Bioenergy is also about an actual interconnection of energy meridians that pervades and surrounds the body. Around each of us is a subtle but real region of radiation, something a skilled bioenergy therapist can use to trace the roots of a physical ailment, and once uncovered, ultimately heal.

Energy healing seems the most mysterious of all non-Western medical treatment. The root cause of all physical and mental illnesses come from an imbalance or a blockage in the flow of the human life energy called the "chi" or "prana." Bioenergetic healing seeks to release blockages and achieve balance to allow physical and mental healing to occur. Skeptics think the healing of the illness is imaginary.

The basis of acupuncture is energetic healing, and it is increasingly covered by medical insurance. Practitioners of modern Western medicine accept acupuncture but do not take it seriously, since they do not believe in the existence of this bioenergy field. They think it works by triggering nerves to release painkillers, not involving energy meridians. Other energy healers work with subtle hand contact or sometimes no physical contact. This form of healing is much less accepted. However, in many cases there is an open-mindedness that if there is no other solution, and it doesn't make things worse, then it's worth a try—even if you don't understand or believe in it.

There is written record as far back as 5,000 B.C. of the concept of a bioenergy field that surrounds every living creature, which provides a template upon which the physical cells grow. A disorder in the energy template will be followed by a disorder in the physical cells. This concept of healing our energetic fields offers some very real and effective answers for anyone lacking relief offered by Western medicine.

Initial understanding of this bioenergy field possibly came from careful experimentation and observation of gestures of hand placement in different situations. Where the hands are placed have been associated with what are known as *chakras*, considered energy centers where we draw our attention and invest our energy either knowingly or unknowingly. The body can be divided into different chakra regions. The illustrations that follow show five of these regions. They show how we as humans have been intuitively mapping this energetic existence in our bodies.

Situation: Hands behind the head to assist thinking for the correct decision. This region covers the fifth and sixth chakras.

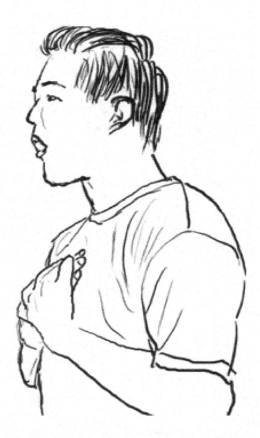

Situation: Hands over heart after witnessing
adorable behavior from child. This covers
the fourth chakra region.

Situation: Hands above navel area while seeking strength after stressful news. This covers the third chakra region.

Situation: Hands held behind back pelvis while
introspecting and reminiscing. Gesture conveys
openness to listen, and that for the moment
judgmental behavior is suspended. A non-
threatening gesture of withholding one's power.

I have shown five chakra regions. A common view of the energy
field involves a total of seven chakras. There are some who believe in
more than seven chakras with different sides, dimensions and layers.
However, I will only focus on the seven chakras most commonly
agreed upon.

Energy Anatomy

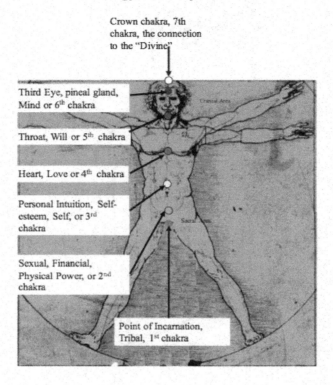

Crown chakra, 7th
chakra, the connection
to the "Divine"

Third Eye, pineal gland,
Mind or 6th chakra

Throat, Will or 5th chakra

Heart, Love or 4th chakra

Personal Intuition, Self-
esteem, Self, or 3rd
chakra

Sexual, Financial,
Physical Power, or 2nd
chakra

Point of Incarnation,
Tribal, 1st chakra

In the above diagram, the arrows point to the seven major chakras. The bottom or first chakra deals with the customs, rules, and traditions you grow into and accept. The second chakra deals with your sexuality, creativity and power, and any blockages here will translate into things such as lower back pain and diseases of the colon and sexual organs. The third chakra lies above your navel and deals with your self-thoughts, self-esteem, and intuition. Any disorders here will translate into feelings of insecurity, stomach disorders, back pain, or other ailments in the mid-section of your body. The fourth chakra deals with love. A disorder here would translate into heart and chest-related problems. The fifth chakra lies in the upper throat region and deals with your will to speak the truth and tend to relate to throat and mouth problems. The sixth chakra is where we see and perceive. Disorders here can translate into self-harming attitudes, concepts, and physical disorders in the brain. The seventh chakra lies at the top of your head and is related to your connection to the Divine. A disorder here translates into a loss of a greater purpose and a spiritual disconnect.

Based upon this, one might think that healing the energetic body can cure everything. The stories of "faith healing" or miracles being performed by saints could be viewed as energetic healing. In fact, the energetic domain at first seemed to be the one view that could integrate tangibles—brain, body, and heart; with intangibles—mind, emotion, love, spirit, and soul. The chakra system shows where to connect with your mind, emotions, love, spirit, and soul.

So, are energy chakras spiritual?

When you hear about subtle force fields or radiation emanating from our bodies, you might think about religious sightings, ghosts, and spirits, and consider energy and spiritual the same. That makes energy related to religion and based upon belief and faith. So you then might feel skeptical that this bioenergetic field with chakras really exists.

I grew up Catholic and was taught that people can be healed and raised from the dead. Therefore, believing that energy was something spiritual was easy. Energetic healing might be the same as evangelistic faith healing. But I had found that my belief in energy healing offered me no more for my life than if I were a skeptic. I'll describe why next.

CHAPTER 4

Energy Healing and Beyond

There was a time many years ago my dearest wife was ill from symptoms that different medical doctors, specialists, and therapists failed to diagnose or address. In a situation where conventional Western medicine was ill equipped to help her, we ultimately found that energy medicine had one of the most potent healing effects. And so, through the healing journey of my wife, I came to believe in holistic wellness through energy healing.

Some energy healing sessions seemed to trigger long-lasting relief. However, with time, I observed that most healing effects wore off, and that repeat sessions would become less effective. It was frustrating and depressing for both of us. What had become clear was that the solution to her physical ailments lay in a deeper understanding of spirituality and how it relates to the physical, mental, and energetic modalities of holistic medicine.

Is energy the basis of all life? Are energy and spirit the same thing? Are soul and spirit the same thing? I read a couple of sources on spirituality that talked about the "seat of your soul" residing in one of the seven chakras. Is spirituality in the mind, the heart, or the physical body? These are philosophical questions that we may toy with in a philosophy class, where the answer is subjective, so there is never a right or wrong answer and no further clarity is given. In my life, getting this clarity was needed, and my frustration drove me to find that clarity.

The bottom line is that in our language we do have synonyms, but still each word is unique in its connotations. *Mind, mental, brain, body, physical, spirit, soul,* and *energy* have overlapping meaning and application, but the nuances are different.

Just what are the differences? The answer requires removing the ambiguity. I've mentioned the mind, body, and spirit division of health and mentioned the mental, physical, and energetic views. Then how do energy and spirit relate? Maybe they are the same.

Maybe energy is the fourth modality of existence when people use the usual buzzwords of mind, body, and spirit.

Energy healers and nuclear scientists see the connection of energy to everything. The difference is that nuclear scientists focus on how immense energy can be released from matter, while energy healers balance subtle amounts of energy within your body, to create physical changes in the mind or the body. Acupuncturists claim to be able to heal all aspects of your body and your life by removing blockages in your Chi.

So one can also view energy as overlapping all three: mind, body, and spirit. For a while this is the view I believed in, and that getting potent energy healing would have provided lasting permanent wellness for my wife. This was not the case. For my wife, healing the mind didn't work, healing the body didn't work, and to great disappointment eventually even healing the energy did not work.

Distinguishing Spirit from Energy

Back in the early 2000s, I was in clinical depression. I neglected my sleep, dropped off my exercise, cared little about my future, and contemplated suicide. I became increasingly likely to do things that provided short-term relief at the expense of my long-term welfare.

Back then I was a caretaker with all my focus on the quest to heal my wife even at the expense of my own well-being. I was not healthy. I felt I did the best I could to help my wife. I truly overextended and exhausted myself. After a long journey of trying the whole gamut of healing that could be found in holistic medicine, there was no solution. It seemed hopeless. I felt like giving up. But if you still don't want to give up, you will ask in total frustration, hopelessness, and powerlessness: "Now what!?" And in that very question of desperation the truth starts to emerge.

Eventually I found that I needed to focus on healing myself first. How the rest of your loved ones heal physically, mentally, emotionally, and socially can be tied to how much you heal yourself. Indeed, how the rest of the world will impact you is tied to your own wellness. How well you evolve and grow in life is very strongly tied to your own inner health. If you are not healthy and well, you will become increasingly negative, causing you to block out options and possibilities and not have the strength to support others in getting better. You might even make the ones you are trying to help worse.

As of this writing in 2019, I can say that my life is so much better than it used to be. However, the change in improvement has been in the form of slow and small steps; often two steps forward and one step back, which over many years added up to large changes. Much of how I've become better is a result of how

I'm able to witness how I've become healthier and as a result know that I've become better. As a result, my life has become better.

During the time I was in clinical depression I also led a spirituality and self-improvement class. In that class I covered some of what I have already covered in this book. There was one day of my class that nobody showed up. Even though my class was empty, I decided to teach. I proceeded to write things I would have written on the chalkboard if people had shown up. What I wrote was flawed, because something was missing that was related to my wellness.

Many times my wife told me that we needed to find the "root cause" of what was going on in her health that no one in current Western or Eastern thoughts of wellness could "cure." I began asking myself what was the "root cause" of physical, mental, and energetic healing not working. Alone in my empty class the answer came to me.

The "root cause" was the spirit. What mental, physical, and even energetic healing therapies were failing at was in the spirit. The un-wellness for my wife, our relationship, and even myself was in the spirit. But in my empty class on spirituality I was further guided to view the spirit with a new kind of insight.

It is important to explain what I precisely mean by the "spirit". I feel that knowing this will lead to the root of all things. Knowing the nature of the spirit is the path to healing oneself of physical, mental, and emotional pains.

Getting Back to Basics

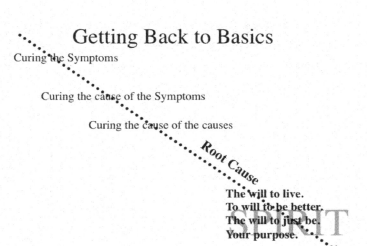

Curing the Symptoms

Curing the cause of the Symptoms

Curing the cause of the causes

Root Cause

The will to live.
To will to be better.
The will to just be.
Your purpose.

SPIRIT

The root of all the physical symptoms and all the physical, mental, and energetic reasons for a person's personal plight were basic issues of willingness to want to get better. Some would call this "intentionality."

Believe it or not, there are advantages in becoming weak and ill. Sometimes acting in a "strong" manner may seem to put you at a disadvantage, and acting in a state of illness or "weakness" may seem to grant you special privileges and power.

At the bottom of the willingness to get better are deep fundamental questions about ourselves, such as, What's the purpose of my life? Does being better mean more money? Time? Freedom? Love? Friends? Why do I want to continue? Why should I bother trying to live a fuller life when it hurts? Why try when I'm afraid? What's the purpose of striving when life keeps knocking me down?

The asking of these kinds of questions are the essence of Spirituality for Real. What dawned upon me was the basic misunderstanding of spirituality. Spirit is not a subset of the part of our human nature; it is everything about our human nature.

Spirit in Everyday Use

Most of us were raised to think of the "spirituality" kind of spirit as something that is always mystical, mysterious, and only the domain of religious leaders, priests, and monks. That is fine and correct if you want things to be like that, but this view will not serve you well.

Step back and observe which uses of the word *spirit* really have shown real-world impact day in and day out. What follows are some examples:

What is SPIRIT?

Team Spirit

Family Spirit   **Creative Spirit**

Human Spirit Winning Spirit

Pioneering Spirit   "Spirit of Cooperation" Olympic Spirit

Innovative Spirit   from G7 Summit Speech

Fighting Spirit   **Living Spirit**

Spirit of Democracy

Spirit of Free Enterprise

In Good Spirits   "A Spirit of Economic Success"
                         from BWI Business Partnership, Inc.

Entrepreneurial Spirit

Spirit of St. Louis

"Economic numbers show spirit"   American Spirit
from Business Section Las Vegas Review-Journal

When you observe how we use the word *spirit* in everyday life, what you first notice is that despite all the use of the word *spirit*, there is often no reference to religion or God. Although religion is a kind of spirituality, it is only a subset of spirituality. Religion is not the whole of spirituality. At its basics, spirit is about the purpose for being. Spirit is the result of people working together for a common cause. Spirit is that common cause.

- Spirit in everyday use is about a greater purpose. It is an overriding force, purpose, or goal that moves individuals to become greater and more important than as individuals. The whole is greater than the sum of the parts because the parts are inspired to be greater than themselves. This is found in: Team Spirit, Creative Spirit, and Family Spirit.

- Spirit is about having meaning and purpose, of getting faith and belief against the odds, and overcoming the odds, even defying logic or reason. This is found in: Winning Spirit, Spirit of St. Louis, and Pioneering Spirit.

- Spirit is about the desire to live, to be, even in bad times. It is what motivates an individual. It is the "contagious" effect that causes an individual to motivate others and others to motivate that individual. This is found in: Living Spirit, Fighting Spirit, and Spirit of Cooperation.

- Spirit is to embrace and build each other up with appreciation, acknowledgement, and love. This is found in: Loving Spirit, Spirit of Democracy, and Olympic Spirit.

This is the meaning of spirit that we use in everyday practical life, and it is the meaning that is real. We have been taught to think that "spirituality" is something more esoteric that has to do with prayer, priests, gurus, yogis, shamans, meditation, altered states, ghosts, voices from the heavens, and miraculous bursts of light. While it can be those things, to think that way exclusively is to put your spirituality at a distance. Bringing spirituality closer means to use the concept of spirit in the everyday sense of Team Spirit, Winning Spirit, Creative Spirit, and Human Spirit.

In religions such as Christianity, Judaism, and Islam the spirit is a "ghostly" existence of ourselves that is located within the body. However, in the larger and more practical sense of spirituality, the spirit is not a location and not something to be studied in an anatomy class. Rather the spirit is the purpose and the reason for this energy aura and physical makeup for existing.

Spirit Encompasses Energetic and Physical

The spirit is not so much a thing as a system. It is a system that is our total being. The spirit, our spirituality, is the "why we exist as we do" in the real world. When we refer to Team Spirit or Human Spirit, we are not referring to ghosts but a system that drives a team or drives a human. For all of us, the root cause we seek lies in healing the system that is the purpose for being. Healing the system gives us the passion to transcend life's challenges.

With this realization, the view of total well-being looks like the diagram that follows.

But there is also the aspect of how energetic healing effectively covers issues related to the state of the mind and body. When I started to combine these concepts, I could see an explanation of the difference and relationship between energy and the spirit. It is the chakra system that pulls everything together, if you look at things initially as divided into two areas, physical and energetic.

	Energetic View	Physical View
7th	Prayer, Divine Inspiration	Crown of Head
6th	Mind	Brain
5th	Voice	Mouth, Throat
4th	Love	Heart
3rd	Self-esteem/Integrity/Instinct	Gut, Stomach
2nd	Sex, Power	Lower Back, Sex Organs
1st	Belonging	Tail Bone, Sacrum

The chakra system is a map that shows how you can understand the mind and all parts of the body by focusing on seven energy centers. The chakra system also explains why energetic healing is effective in addressing almost everything. This is exactly what I observed. The final missing piece was understanding that the entire chakra system itself was encompassed by the spirit.

	Energetic View	Physical View
7th	Prayer, Divine Inspiration	Crown of Head
6th	Mind	Brain
5th	Voice	Mouth, Throat
4th	Love	Heart
3rd	Self-esteem/Integrity/Instinct	Gut, Stomach
2nd	Sex, Power	Lower Back, Sex Organs
1st	Belonging	Tail Bone, Sacrum

Under this realization, the spirit is the whole, and it can be divided into physical and energetic. The physical-bodily existence

is as much a part of the spiritual world as the energetic-bodily existence. If we define the mind as our thoughts, ideas, and perceptions,
and if we define the brain as the physical connection to our mind,
then our mental existence can be seen as having two parts: the
physical, which is the brain; and the energetic, which is the mind.

A person must address his physical health, energetic health, and
overall purpose of how and why everything works together. The
overall purpose of how and why is the spirit. Neglect the physical
and you will weaken the energetic; neglect the energetic and you
will weaken the physical. Weaken either the physical or energetic
and you weaken the spirit. Neglect the spirit and you weaken the
underlying cause and purpose for better physical and energetic
health. They are all connected, and you must learn to understand
and believe it not just in your mind but also in your heart and soul.

Spirit Means Purpose

Now.

Understand.

The spirituality I am speaking of is about your life. You have been taught to believe so much in the physical world. Many of you are starting to be introduced to the energetic healing world. But truly none of these worlds matters much if you don't have the spiritual.

I make it a point to stop you, Reader, right here and right now because I want you to start to tap into the place that inspires everyday people to achieve seemingly superhuman feats and to experience places of overwhelming joy, abundance, and happiness. From now on, when you read or hear the word *Spirit*, when you hear the word *Spirituality*, I want you to think the word *PURPOSE*.

Remember. SPIRIT = PURPOSE.

And then when you think of PURPOSE, I want you to think about:

1. Your purpose as defined in the past. Ask yourself why have you come here?

2. Your purpose as defined in the present moment. Ask yourself why do you still exist here?

3. Your purpose as defined in the future. Ask yourself what is it that is needed for you to be complete?

We must address an aspect of the spirit to answer these questions. The word *spirit* can mean "the reason why many people decide to work together as a team." However, I want to focus on the meaning of the word *spirit* to answer why you decide to be who you are.

Before we continue I ask you to remember: SPIRIT = PURPOSE.

CHAPTER 5

What's the Soul?

U p to this point, I have described a way of relating to mind, body, energy, and spirit. The spirit encompasses the energetic and physical views of the way to address issues in the mind and body, but another word is also commonly addressed, and that is *soul*. There are phrases such as "Nurturing the Soul" and "Feeding the Soul." *Soul* is a word that is commonly found in everyday life, so it must be important. Where and how does the soul fit in?

Maybe the soul is the spirit. You commonly hear phrases such as "Winning Spirit," "Team Spirit," or "In the Spirit of Peace." If the Soul and Spirit are the same, then why don't we use terms like "Winning Soul," "In the Soul of Peace," and "Team Soul"? The word *soul* has a different meaning and intent than spirit, even though addressing the soul is very spiritual. Is the soul the same as or different from the spirit?

In Christianity, the soul is thought of as our "ghostly" essence without the physical body. It makes us unique; it breathes life into a physical body. It is what will remain after death. Christianity also thinks of the spirit the same way. However, if the practical context of spirit as in "Team Spirit" is different from this religious context of spirit as in "ghostly essence," it's not accurate to say spirit and soul are the same. What remains true about the concept of the word *soul* even if you're not religious, is that the soul is about our deeper identity and our truest essence.

In Buddhism, the soul is thought not to exist except as an illusion. Buddhism is concerned about the purpose and cause of pain and suffering. Buddhists understand pain and suffering to be the result of our ego, which gives us a unique identity, a separateness without which we would be one with everything and reach a state of nirvana. Our soul is about being unique and separate, and so for as long as we refuse to surrender it, this becomes the source of pain and suffering. Under the concept of reincarnation, if one fails to reach nirvana, then one necessarily remains as a separate individual and retains the illusion of the soul. With one's soul intact, one is yet again not fully awakened and will ultimately seek to reincarnate. Upon reincarnation, any pains that were not resolved in a past life will persist in the new life. If and when we finally awaken, the illusion of the soul will disappear and we shall be one with Buddha. Therefore, in the Buddhist concept of the non-existence of a soul, we shed some light on the nature of the soul. We still come out with the concept that the soul is about giving us a unique identity and our individual existence.

To add a further twist, there is a concept of a "seat of the soul"—where the soul might actually sit. Philosopher Emanuel Swedenborg gives a most explicit opinion of this seat of the soul. In the eighteenth century, Swedenborg wrote many books on physiology and psychology, and as he became more interested in the relationship between science and religion, his interests began to focus on the mystery of soul–body interaction. Swedenborg saw the human brain as the seat of our soul.

Barbara Brennan, a well-known energetic healer who sees human energy fields and chakras, states that the "seat of the soul" has to do with our soul's longing. Barbara says that this seat of the soul lies in the proximity of the upper heart region.

In the book *The Seat of the Soul*, Gary Zukav encourages us to think of the body seated in a soul rather than a soul within a body, and states that each soul comes to the Earth with gifts. A soul incarnates to heal, to balance its energy, to pay its karmic debts, and complete the tasks of a contract which, when complete, will enrich the soul. Each soul takes upon itself the completion of particular tasks in a contract with the Universe. All the experiences of your life serve to awaken within you the memory of that contract and to prepare you to fulfill it. Zukav says the seat of your soul is the source of your creativity and authentic power, referring to it as the source of ego energy.

Zukav is not explicit about a specific location in the body to find the soul, but rather states that intuition is the "walkie-talkie" to the soul. Our life's goal is to use that walkie-talkie to align our personality with the contract of our soul. In energetic healing, intuition resides in the third chakra region. This view tends to have a commonality with all prior views of the soul, in that the soul is a unique self with unique gifts. In energetic healing the third chakra is about issues of self-esteem, intuition, and personal integrity.

Therefore, with all these different views, where does this soul reside?

Where is the Soul?

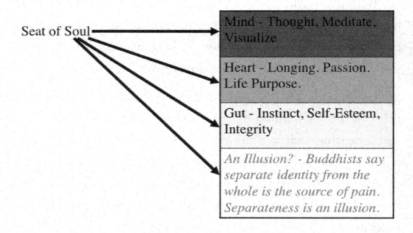

My intuition says that it is inaccurate to state that the entire soul sits on one particular chakra. It's more appropriate to think of the soul as an existence that draws upon one or more of the chakras in feeling itself, to make itself complete. The chakras are important only in their location because they help define the physical body. If we had no physical body, there would be little need for chakras. Each chakra, then, is a path to the soul.

My intuition also says that it is accurate to consider one chakra as the dominant path to the soul. Therefore, we are expressing where we see our soul predominantly seated when saying the "seat of the soul." Are we more intellect or more heart? When you are seated in a chair, you don't mean that all of you is where you touch the chair; it's just that the center of your body mass is planted in the chair. Your head, feet, and hands don't sit in the chair; your dominant part, the center of your body mass, does.

In physics, to most effectively change the motion of a moving body, you should apply force as close as possible to its center of gravity. In American football, a person wishing to tackle a runner most effectively should tackle the runner's center of gravity. For the human body, the center of gravity is around the midsection. If you tackle higher, the runner may fall but will slide under you. If you tackle lower, the runner will trip but stumble over you; tackle the midsection of the runner, and the runner will stop and drop. The midsection is recognized as the foundation for power in martial arts, boxing, pitching, swimming, and running.

Under this concept of a predominant place most effective in connecting to your soul or the "seat of the soul," this same midsection area is most effective way to connect with the soul. In terms of chakras, this most corresponds to the third chakra. While all chakras are paths to the soul, the third chakra is the dominant path.

You may wonder why I devote time to physically locating the soul in the body. I'm interested in telling you about connecting with your spirit, and more specifically the spirit that is specific to just you. Once you learn to find and sustain that connection to your spirit, you will tap into tremendous strength, courage, energy, and happiness. You will feel this physically and not merely understand it as an abstraction in the mind. The spirit that is specific to you is not mental hocus-pocus. If that's all you choose to think, it will not serve you well.

The physical world is a very big part of the spiritual world, but there is also an energetic world that is also a big part of the spiritual world. I must address the physical and the energetic if I am to address the spirit. I am now trying to focus on that aspect of your purpose that is specific to your individuality and existence, to focus on your soul, and to look at it from:

1. The purpose of your soul (Remember SPIRIT = PURPOSE)
2. The physical connections to your soul and
3. The energetic connections to your soul.

In all three senses of finding the connection to your soul, it's best to look at some of our everyday use of the word *soul*. Read the following:

The Seat of the Soul?

Running for the Soul

Feeding the Soul

Soul Music   Nourishing the Soul

You've got Soul

Soul Food

Chicken Soup for the Soul®

Searching your Soul

Sense the difference in the emotions and tone of the phrases compared to how we might use the words for spirit, for thought, and for love. What stands out in the use of the word *soul* is this sense of digging down, finding an essence, a nourishing, a recharging, a sense of just you, and a sense of reconnecting with who you are.

Feel Your Soul

I have explained that the third chakra is the dominant connection with your soul. Most likely you may view this as only an interesting concept of the mind. I'd like to help you understand this idea at a more intuitive level and actually start to feel where your soul is. Let's try to feel the sensations in our body in the third, fourth, and sixth chakras, and see where the "seat of the soul" seems to most resonate.

Focus on the sixth chakra, the mind. If I say dig into your soul, do I mean dig into your intellect? Does your head start to hurt with too much intellectual stuff when you dig deep? Notice the appeal to use food connotations with our soul? Do we instinctively feel hunger in the brain area?

Focus on the fourth chakra, the heart. The heart and love do have stronger connections to the soul. The power of love is such a great and absolute force. Ultimately, love is at the center of all things, including all of the other chakras. So one might think that love and the heart is the seat of the soul. However, we must still acknowledge that *heart* and *soul* are different words. These two words aren't synonyms in the dictionary. There must be some reason why humanity sensed these words were different.

The best understanding is to consider a situation where you feel threatened. Maybe you have watched a horror movie and are walking home alone at night, frightened of being mugged by a monster. Maybe at your office workplace you're intimidated by a personal visit from the company CEO whom you've never met.

Also consider situations where your psyche is threatened. Maybe there is a person you are jealous of who seems to get everything they want and does everything right. You talk to yourself about how this person is really not so great and that you could be so much better if you had the same breaks. And then this person does something gracious for you that makes you feel small for being jealous. Maybe you've put great pride and effort into a project at work and then someone who knows little about your effort criticizes your work and you feel ignored, hurt and angry.

I bring up these kinds of situations because they are threats to your personal security, your sense of self-esteem, your sense of pride, and your sense of integrity. In all of these situations, where was the hurt? Where was the predominant physical sensation of tightness? Is it in your head, your heart, or your gut? You will find in such stress we most commonly feel it in the stomach area, the third chakra area.

Interestingly though, through all these situations where does the answer to overcome this tightness arise? Your heart. For when you learn to start following the heart, you start feeling glowing warmth in the heart that enables you to let go of the tightness in your gut. The gut concerns itself with your fear or pain. It's the heart that provides the courage that can dissipate the fear and pain.

Think of someone who is important to you, such as the one who you love the most in your life, your "soulmate," a family member, a pet, or a best friend. Now imagine that person is lost inside a very scary haunted house. Imagine the most precious person in your life has about four hours to live unless you find him or her. Notice how the fear is put into a much different perspective when the stakes are higher.

If you run away you might live the rest of your life in comfort, but there will always be this ache of regret over the loss of your deepest love. Inevitably, you will find yourself driven to brave that haunted house because the risk of losing this most precious person in your life far outweighs being frightened by ghosts. The pain of living without love, with an ache in the heart, is much greater than experiencing the pain, fear, and tightness in the gut.

Let's bring the focus back to the soul and the third chakra. I want you to consider the gut region because I want you to connect on an instinctive level. Next time when you meditate, consider that region of your body because this is going to be key to tapping into your soul. When you tap into the gut region you're communicating at an instinctive level with your soul. It's one thing to agree intellectually upon your purpose in life, but it's another to know your purpose so innately that it's as undeniable as needing air to breathe. You can come to an intellectual conclusion that you need to breathe air to live, but if you are drowning in water and fighting for breath, you come to know instinctively that you need to breathe to live.

Consider feelings of shame and embarrassment and consider your physical discomforts. Do you have stomach ulcers? Do you ever lose your appetite? Do you ever find yourself feeling empty or bored and so you eat to fill the void? Are you embarrassed about the appearance of your gut? Do you cry or ache deep within your gut? Does your back ache? Do you have digestive or intestinal disorders? Understand that these physical connections relate to the "seat of your soul." When you understand the physical connection, also know the energetic connection behind it. Know about the third chakra.

Touch the physical sensations of the gut. Connect with the energetic intent of this third chakra region and you will be caressing warm hands around your soul. Once you physically and energetically nurture this region, you will find yourself better able to mentally read the message of your soul. Once you are able to read those messages, you will know your path to completion. Once you know and align with this path, you will be energized, courageous, thriving, and happy. There will be no need for ulcers, no pain or crying from the gut, and no issue of self-esteem around the gut. You will emotionally and physically begin to manifest the outward image of vivacity and vitality because your outside will reflect the bright shining light that is showering from within.

So now, know this. Your soul is that aspect of the spirit that defines your individuality, your separateness from complete and total happiness. Your soul is a living, breathing spiritual contract to achieve happiness, where each clause is some aspect of yourself that you find lacking to make yourself complete. I talked about Spirit being equated to PURPOSE, and now I'm saying that the soul is about your specific purpose. Your soul is the reason for and answer to:

1. **The Past:** Why you had to go through what you went through.

2. **The Present:** Why you are in the state and situation you are in here and now.

3. **The Future**: What you must still experience to be complete and what you must do to fulfill your purpose.

Touch and focus on the physical region of your gut. Touch and focus on the third chakra and its intent. Then discover the terms of this spiritual contract about why you are here and why you are experiencing your current circumstances and situations. When you do this, you are actively reading the terms of your contract, but in an instinctive kind of language. When you read the terms of your contract, you will find that they are both clear and binding. Like it or not, you are bound to fulfill the terms of your contract, but just the same you are also inevitably assured to succeed in fulfilling it. Know these terms and you will tap into endless energy and understand the extent of their inevitable binding. Focus on feeling the gut area and begin to nurture the intent of your third chakra and finally heal the physical aspects of your gut.

Complete the terms of your contract, and your soul is complete. Upon completion, the soul starts to lose its need to be unique. That aspect of your spirit that makes you unique starts to become one with the Universe. As your soul surrenders its need to exist, you get in exchange confidence, security, and unity.

WakundaMa® Yoga: Meditation

To help you become better acquainted with your chakras and most importantly the third chakra and its connection to your soul, I encourage you to try this meditation I call the "Crying Meditation." Beginners to meditation are often challenged because their mind will drift with day-to-day chatter. This meditation prevents your mind from drifting by keeping you occupied with generating sound, feeling sensations, and visualizing locations. Your physical body and emotional feelings will also be engaged. The result is increased mental focus, opening to self-healing, and continued alignment with universal truth.

PREPARING FOR CRYING MEDITATION

a. As preparation, please think of any uncomfortable or painful situation that has threatened your self-esteem. This could be in the present or past when you worried about something not going your way, about failing, about loss. These are situations of insecurity or self-doubt, when others criticized your faults or asked why you can't be more like someone else. Focus on just one of these situations and use this meditation to heal and nourish this area of your life.

b. Dress in comfortable clothes and find a quiet area; find a room where no one can hear you.

c. I want you to remember three chakras areas: the top, middle, and bottom. They are as follows: the top or seventh chakra is at the top of your head; the middle or third chakra will be just above your navel; and the bottom or first chakra is at the very bottom of your torso.

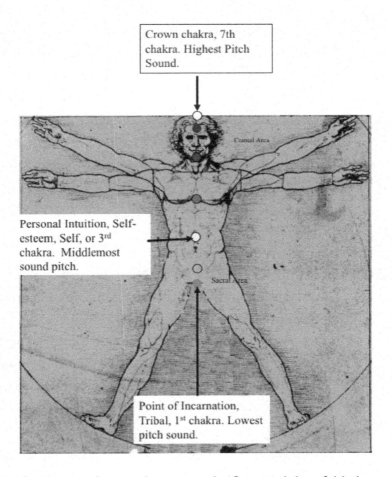

Crown chakra, 7th chakra. Highest Pitch Sound.

Personal Intuition, Self-esteem, Self, or 3rd chakra. Middlemost sound pitch.

Point of Incarnation, Tribal, 1st chakra. Lowest pitch sound.

d. Sit upright in a chair or on the floor with legs folded.

e. Keep your eyes open first so you can read the meditation. When you have memorized it you can close your eyes.

PREPARING VOICE FOR CRYING MEDITATION

The goal of this meditation is to start associating lower-pitched sounds with the lower parts of the body and higher-pitched sounds with the higher parts of the body. In music, to help someone sing the seven notes of the music scale, people are often trained to sing different, word like sounds at different pitches. However, for this exercise I'll make it easy. You will learn to sing with only one word "La" as in "La La La" Try singing "La La La" as low as you can until it's too low to make any sound. Men will tend to find the lower pitches easier. Women will tend to find the higher pitches easier. Try raising the pitch of your "La La La" until it get almost squeaky and falsetto and your voice cracks and can no longer make a sound. This singing will then turn into an exercise in crying. You have been taught how not to cry and so this is a lesson on how to cry deep as you once did as an infant.

DOING CRYING MEDITATION

1. Lowest tone. Please make that lowest tone. Sing a low tone by singing the word *Laaaaaah* as long as you can and as low as possible. Now choose to associate the lowest possible tone you can make with your first chakra. Understand I'm not telling you it's a fact the first chakra is the lowest tone; I'm telling you just to exercise your right to choose this to be correct.

2. Highest pitch tone. Please make the highest pitch tone. Sing *Laaaaaaaaah* in the highest pitch possible without raising your volume. This will be way up in the falsetto regions of your voice. Now I want you to associate this pitch of tone with the top chakra located at the top of your head.

3. Repeat lowest tone: Now really try the lowest tone to be really low, until your voice fades into an airy sounding whisper. This shall be the tone of the lowest chakra, your bottom chakra.

4. Repeat highest tone: Now really try to get the highest high, until you voice cracks into a falsetto or squeaky whisper. This shall be the tone of the highest chakra, your top chakra.

5. Now go from highest tone gradually down to the lowest tone. This means you will hit pitches between the highest and lowest pitch you can sing. After you hit your lowest tone make your voice gradually rise in pitch until you reach your highest pitched tone.

6. Now with the sound *Laaaaaaaaaaaaah* I want you to start homing in on the middle-most range between your lowest and highest pitch. It should be the tone you can hit most easily because it is exactly in the middle of your range. This is the tone I want you to associate with the middle chakra that is a point near your navel.

7. Now fine-tune that middle range of tone. Try increasing the pitch of your *Laaaaaah* slightly, then decrease it slightly. Keep going up and down in pitch just slightly until you sense that you feel the sound most resonating with that point just above your navel.

8. Now recall a pain or discomfort that has to do with your self-worth, self-confidence, self-security, and self-purpose that you would like to begin healing. This is not so much physical pain but emotional like a moment of deep humiliation, embarrassment, frustration, loneliness, defeat, worthlessness, and hopelessness.

9. Touch into that pain or need and sing out *Laaaaaaaaaaaaaaaaaaaah* into that middle-most range of you voice that resonates most with that middle chakra. Sing *Laaaaaaaaaaaaaaaaaaaaaah* as long as you can until

there is "no air" in your lungs. And by no air I really mean vacate the tiniest pockets of air in your lungs. This is singing transformed into crying.

10. When there is no air left and you need to breathe, fill your lungs as full as possible. Hold your breath and count to three, and then try to breath in even more air. Try to fill out the tiniest pockets of your lungs with air.

11. Again touch into that pain or discomfort at the precise moment where it was or is most intense and sing out *Laaaaaaaaaaaaaaaaaaaaaaaaaah* at the right pitch so it's centered in the middle range of your body. Keep singing out *Laaaaaaaaaaaah* in one breath until you thoroughly and completely empty your lungs.

12. Now let's alter the sound. Change the *Laaaaaaaaaaaaah* to a *Laaaaaaaaaaauumm*. Again, touch into that pain or discomfort at the moment where it was or is most intense and cry *Laaaaaaaaaaaaaaaaaaaaaaauummmmm* at the right pitch so it's centered in the middle range of your body. Keep singing out *Laaaaaaaaaaaaaaaaaaaauummmmm* in one breath until you thoroughly and completely empty your lungs.

13. Change sound to *Aaaaaaaaaaaaaaaaaaaaaaaaaaaaaaaauummmmmm*. Touch into that pain or discomfort at the precise moment in time where it was or is most intense and cry *Aaaaaaaaaaaaaaaaaaaaaaauummmmm* at the right pitch so it's centered in the middle range of your body. Keep singing out *Aaaaaaaaaaaaaaaaaaauummmmm* in one breath without stopping until you absolutely run out of the last drop of air in your lungs.

14. Repeat this as often as desired, and for each cry you will better learn to release the pain that for so long has begged your attention to be nurtured.

15. As you do this meditation you will find you can cry softer and softer in volume until no one else can hear you. You can cry in a whisper of your breath and have the same effect as long as the intent of the cry is as genuine as if you were audibly. Master this exercise and you can do this meditation silently at any moment, whether standing in the middle of a crowd or sitting in a car.

Note that you can find a recording guiding you through this mediation at the website wakundama.com

WakundaMa® Yoga: Physical Movement

Another way of helping you get familiar with the chakras is by mastering circular motions across each chakra. This technique is based upon a widespread physical therapy exercise known broadly as the "pelvic clock," but here we extend it to of all seven chakra regions. In so doing we end up covering the spine. The end result is not only increased familiarity with the chakras but a method of relieving back pain and tension.

PREPARING FOR CHAKRA ROTATIONS

First lie on your back on a cushioned surface such as a yoga mat or a carpet. Bend up your knees with feet flat on floor. Notice that that your lower back has a curved part that does not touch the floor. This is the "small" of your back. By rocking your pelvis forward or backward, you can increase the spacing of the small of your back or flatten out it more against the floor. When you are not intentionally trying to rock your pelvis forward or backward, you will naturally relax in a neutral position.

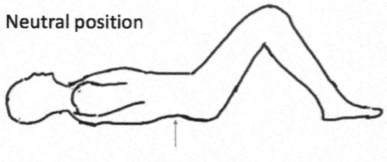

Neutral position

"small" of the back

From the neutral position, rock your pelvis forward and press your tailbone into the floor. The illustration below shows that when you do this, the small of your back arches farther from the floor.

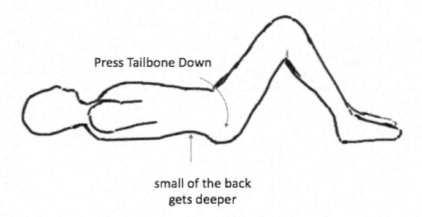

Press Tailbone Down

small of the back
gets deeper

Now rock your pelvis all the way to the opposite direction. Press the middle of your back into the floor. The picture below shows that when you do this, it flattens the small of your back.

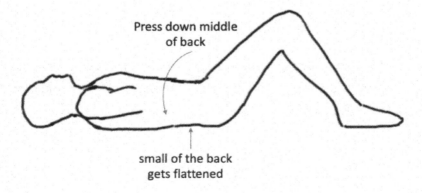

Press down middle
of back

small of the back
gets flattened

Now that we've started to get familiar with the sensation of rocking forward and pressing the tail bone into the floor, and then rocking back and pressing the midback into floor, let's start adding more precision to our motion. Let's start by imagining a clock on the floor facing up. Then lie down on this imaginary clock face with the small of your back in the center of the clock face, and your body oriented so that the 6 is closer to your feet and 12 is closer to your head. This would make 3 lie on your left side and 9 on your right side.

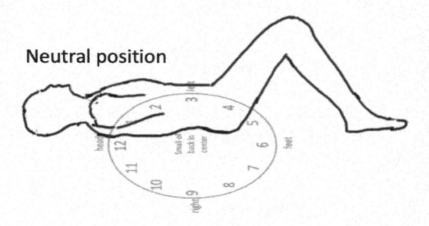

Neutral position

In the picture above, we see the small of our back in center of clock with the number 12 nearer to the head and the number 6 nearer to the feet. Next let's press the tailbone into the floor.

6 o'clock position

Press Tail Bone Down

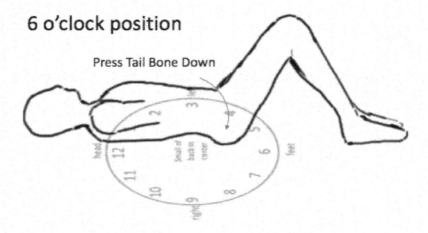

In the figure above, now we can see that with the tail bone pressed down and the pelvis rocked forward we are pointed to the 6 on the clock. Now rock back to neutral, and then press middle of back into floor.

12 o'clock position

Press down middle of back

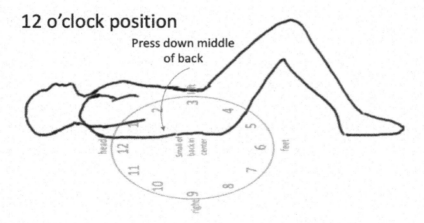

In the picture above, we can see that as we rock the pelvis back and press the middle of back into floor we are pointing to the number 12 on the clock. To point to the 9 on the clock, return to neutral and tilt pelvis to the right. To point to the 3 on the clock, tilt the pelvis to the left.

DOING CHAKRA ROTATIONS: LYING DOWN

Now we are ready to start physically experiencing the chakras by associating with circular motions.

1. First return to neutral and touch every number of the clock. First tilt toward 12, then 1, then 2, then 3, 4, 5, 6, 7, 8, 9, 10, 11, and finally back to 12. You have completed a single rotation clockwise. Now tilt towards 11, 10, 9, 8, 7, 6, 5, 4, 3, 2, 1, and back to 12. You have completed a single rotation counterclockwise.

2. Now go slowly clockwise, but this time make the circle as smooth and perfectly circular as possible. You may have to make the circle smaller or larger to make the circle smoother. Keep experimenting going clockwise but trying your best to make the roundest circle possible.

3. You may notice that certain parts of the circle need more smoothing. For example, say between 9 and 12 needs smoothing out. To smooth out, go to position 9 and then 10, and then 11 and finally 12, and then go back to 11, 10, and finally 9. Go back and forth between 9 and 12 until you like its roundness.

4. Now continue clockwise rotations until you find another area of the clock circle that needs more smoothing out. Then repeat going back and forth on that part of the clock you want to make more round. Keep searching for other parts of the clock circle to round out and repeat. When you are satisfied, complete one full circle clockwise and notice

the improved circularity and roundness of the entire circle you are creating with your rotations.

Now go slowly counterclockwise and try to make the circle smooth and perfectly circular. Experiment with the size of the circle. As you do this exercise more, you'll find that smaller circles will tend to be easier to make more round.

If you find that any part of the circular motion needs more rounding, then pause there and go back and forth, clockwise and counterclockwise. When you are satisfied, complete one full circle counterclockwise and notice the improved circularity and roundness of the entire circle you are creating with your rotations.

You are now mastering a simple yet powerful technique for loosening tightness in the lower back and easing up lower back pain. In this process it's the concentration on making smooth circles going clockwise or counterclockwise that educates your muscles to ease up. This also introduces you to rotating around the second chakra region.

Imagine you can spin your second chakra clockwise or counterclockwise by the way you rotate your pelvis around the clock on the floor. By the way, once you learn how to do this on the floor, you can practice while sitting upright in a chair. Note that this is a great way of helping ease back tightness if you're in a plane or bus seat for long periods of time. You can even do this while standing in line. You can make the circles smaller and less noticeable. As you practice, you can make the circles small enough that they are unnoticed by other people.

Next, place your hand on your belly below the naval. As you rotate your pelvis in a circle, notice how your hand follows the tilting of your belly that is, in turn, following the rotation moments.

This is the sensation of your belly guiding how your hand tilts. Now reverse the sensation. Tilt and rotate your hand allowing the belly to follow the tilt. Observe how your body follows in rotation.

Now you're experiencing the sensation of the hand being the guide that rotates your body through the same clockwise and counterclockwise rotation we started before we involved using the hand as a guide. Just as easily, you can change perspective and have your body and pelvis take the lead again and rotate around the clock and then allow the hand to follow.

Get familiar with the perspective of the pelvis rotations making your belly and hand tilt, and then the reverse of your hand tilting around and allowing your belly and pelvis to follow the hand, all the time keeping the same overall motion. An outside observer won't be able to tell if it's your pelvis leading how the hand tilts or if it's the hand that's leading how the pelvis rotates. Only you will know.

5.　All this time we've had the small of your back in the center of the circle. Now imagine the center of the clock higher up your back by 3 inches. Try making the clockwise and counterclockwise motion 3 inches higher up your body. Adjust the size of the circle for comfort and ease. Generally you'll find it easier to keep circles small in this area. Initially it may be awkward to rotate from this area, so you can place your hand above your navel and below your rib cage to help you feel where the center of the circles should be. Allow your hand to be the guide that tilts and rocks clockwise rotations and tilt and rocks counterclockwise rotations. Concentrate on making the circles as round and smooth as possible in the clockwise direction. If there is any part of the circle you need to smooth out more, feel free to concentrate by going back and forth as needed to smooth out that part of the circle. When you are satisfied with the roundness of the clockwise direction, repeat the process in trying to get as round in counterclockwise circles as possible. When you are done, you are starting to feel out the third chakra area.

6. Now move the center of the clock up your body so that the circles you make are now centered where your heart is. You can move your hand to the center of the chest as a guide. Go clockwise, trying to make the circles as round as possible. Then go counterclockwise, trying to make the circles as round as possible. Adjust the size of the circle for comfort and ease. Pause as needed to go back and forth on any part of the circle to smooth out. This gets you familiar with the fourth chakra.

7. Now move the center of the circles to around your chin. You can move your hand on your chin as a guide. You are rocking your chin clockwise and then counterclockwise. Once again, work on perfecting the roundness of the circles in the clockwise and counterclockwise directions. This starts to emphasize the fifth chakra.

8. Place the center of the circular motion in the middle of your forehead. You can move your hand on top of the center of your forehead. With the help of your hand as a guide, rock your forehead in clockwise and then counterclockwise circles. Once again, work on perfecting the roundness of the circles in the clockwise and clockwise directions. This starts to emphasize the sixth chakra.

9. Now we are going to put it all together and start doing our chakra rotations from our head and working our way down the body. Start with making a single clockwise circle at the sixth chakra (forehead). Next move the circle down to the fifth chakra area (chin) and make a clockwise circle. In turn, make clockwise circles at the fourth chakra region (heart), third chakra (above the navel but below ribcage), and finally at the second chakra region (below naval).

10. Now let's work our way up the body. First, make a counterclockwise circle at the second chakra, then the third chakra, then the fourth chakra, then the fifth, and finally the sixth. You have just made a spiral of counterclockwise circles going up your spine.

11. Now let's work our way back down the body. First make a clockwise circle at the sixth chakra region. Next at the fifth chakra, and then the fourth chakra, and then the third chakra, and finally at your second chakra. You have just made a spiral of clockwise circles going down your spine.

12. You can change things up by making clockwise circles spiral up your spine and then making counterclockwise circles spiral down your spine.

Feel free to experiment and explore all the areas of your entire body from your tailbone to your forehead. As you do this, you draw upon the strength of many thousands of years of association of physical body to energetic chakras. You simultaneously, continually reeducate all the muscles in your body from tail to head, which tends to ease any tension and pain along the entire length of the spine.

Note that a video demonstration of the above motions can be found at the website wakundama.com

DOING CHAKRA ROTATIONS: STANDING

Once you've mastered the chakra rotations lying on the floor, you can next do this standing with knees slightly bent. While standing you can make the circles at any point between your tailbone and forehead as if you were lying down.

When you can do this standing, now you can experience the first chakra. The first chakra is located in the crotch area where your two legs meet. When standing, the first chakra points downward from the bottom of your spine straight into the ground.

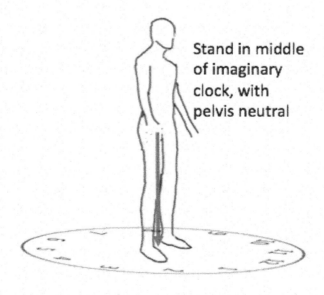

Stand in middle of imaginary clock, with pelvis neutral

Imagine a paintbrush long enough to reach from the crotch to the floor and imagine you are standing on top of that clock face with the number 12 in front of you and number 6 behind you.

1. Now thrust your pelvis forward so that that imaginary paintbrush is pointing at 12, as shown below

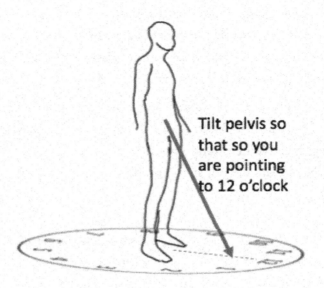

Tilt pelvis so that so you are pointing to 12 o'clock

2. Now thrust back so that your buttocks point to 6 as shown below

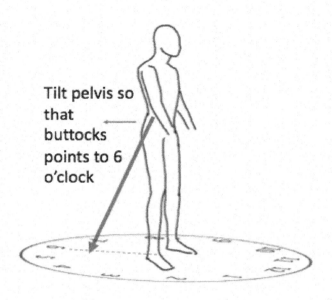

Tilt pelvis so that buttocks points to 6 o'clock

3. Next point to 12, then 1, 2, 3, 4, 5, 6, 7, 8, 9, 10, 11 and back to 12. When you do this motion, you are essentially circling your hips. You have successfully rotated your first chakra through a clockwise rotation. Next try counterclockwise. Work to make the circle as round as possible in both clockwise and counterclockwise directions. Try experimenting with the size of the circle as well. This completes the process of feeling the first chakra.

4. Next, let's get familiar with the seventh chakra, which is at the very top of your head. Imagine a paintbrush going from top of your head pointed straight to the sky.

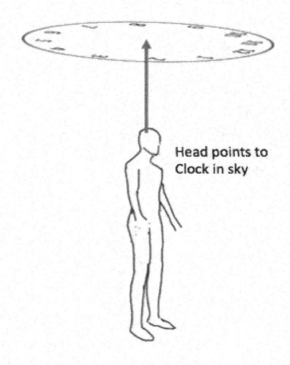

Head points to Clock in sky

5. Tilting your head forward points to 12 o'clock, to the right points to 3, to the back 6 and to the left 9. Rock the top of your head around to create perfect circles in the sky going clockwise and then counterclockwise. This completes your physical association with the seventh chakra.

Now let's put everything together while standing.

6. Make a clockwise circle at the first chakra by painting a circle on the floor.

7. Place your hand on the second chakra (below naval and slightly above groin) and make a clockwise circle just as you would have if you were lying on the ground.

8. Move hand up to third chakra (area between naval and bottom of ribs) and circle clockwise as if you would have if lying on the ground.

9. Move hand to the fourth chakra (middle of chest) and circle clockwise as if you would have if lying on the ground.

10. Place hand on your chin and move your chin in a clockwise circle. You have rotated your fifth chakra.

11. Hand to forehead, rotate your head from the forehead in a clockwise circle. You have rotated your sixth chakra clockwise.

12. Place your hand on top of head to help rotate the top of your head clockwise. You are also rotating that imaginary paintbrush creating circles in the sky.

13. Rotate the top of your head counterclockwise.

14. Move to the sixth chakra and rotate counterclockwise.

15. Move to the fifth chakra and rotate counterclockwise.

16. Move to the fourth chakra and rotate counterclockwise.

17. Move to the third chakra and rotate counterclockwise.

18. Move to the second chakra and rotate counterclockwise.

19. Finally focus on the first chakra and move that imaginary paintbrush in a counterclockwise rotation.

Experiment going from the first chakra and moving up the spine to the seventh chakra but with counterclockwise circles. Experiment moving from the seventh chakra back to the first with clockwise circles. Experiment with the size of the circles. Take time at various points to perfect the roundness of the circles.

As you master this, you can learn to do this with small discrete circles to stay in touch with your chakras as well as benefit from the muscular reeducation and tension release throughout the entire body. I've found this a wonderful technique of loosening up tension throughout body if I find myself standing for long periods of time. It's a technique that can be done with very small circles so that you can do this in public without anyone noticing. You also strengthen and align with the chakra energy system paradigm that has existed for thousands of years. Enjoy!

The collection of the Crying Meditation and these Chakra Rotations are part of WakundaMa® Yoga. You can find videos that guide you through the use of the WakundaMa® Yoga Chakra Rotations in lying, seated, and standing positions at the website wakundama. com

Additionally, demonstrations of applying WakundaMa® Yoga Chakra Rotations to movement and dancing can also be found at wakundama.com

CHAPTER 6
Spirit is Eternal

Your spirit is eternal. While your physical body can bleed, grow old, and die, your spirit will live on, with or without your physical body. As living creatures on this Earth, most are ultimately driven to procreate in order to live on beyond what we can do within just our own bodies. We live on in our children. Not that our physical bodies continue to live on without us, but our spirit and our purpose do.

Knowing that our purpose lives on even without our physical bodies is comforting to us. In fact, if it were a choice of eternal physical life or eternal spiritual existence within others, many might prefer the latter. Why? Because many of us are dissatisfied with what we are physically now and what we have accomplished in this life and may wish we could redo some things.

When we were young and wide-eyed, our spirit was a template for the future and a clean slate with limitless potential. Within others we can see our spirit live on vicariously, still untainted in its potential. As long as that spirit can exist and breathe on, still untainted, we are comforted and pleased, even if it lives on beyond ourselves.

Are there moments when you feel overwhelmed with life? Are there moments in your life when you then feel empty with no purpose? Do you ever wish you were like someone else, but that someone else seems so beyond your capability? Do you ever wish you were wealthier or lived in a different place? Are there times you feel as if everyone is mocking you or shunning you? Do you ever feel alone? Do you ever feel certain people keep hounding or nagging you?

Think about those moments that you felt so frail, so sick, so meek, so weak, so small, so unloved, so unwanted, so ignored, so overlooked, and so less than. These are the vulnerable moments where it is important to remember your eternity. Knowing that your spirit is eternal is powerful. It is also necessary. I say necessary because inevitably, you will have no choice but to acknowledge your eternity, your spirit, if you seek to find wholeness and happiness. If it were not so, you would not have existed.

- **Know that the big things you can wish to accomplish here on earth are really small things.**

- **Know that the small things you do with great love are huge things.**

- **Know that external acts of becoming wealthy, famous, and admired during the approximately 100 years you will exist on Earth will be tiny compared to the history of events in the billions of years of Earth's existence.**

- **Know that each moment you've expressed genuine love, patience, and caring are what becomes immense.**

When you become frustrated because you are working hard to be successful and happy on Earth and not quite getting there, you can step back and smile because it doesn't matter, because you can feel a shining light of confidence within you. Know that the miracles in life are not so much the magical healings from cancer but rather the tiny spark of hope that creates purpose in the times when life seems glum and miserable.

This creates not just purpose but happiness and love even in the midst of apparent defeat and death. In the darkest moments, when all your prayers seem unanswered, when all your rivals seem to achieve victories, when all seem to mock you and your integrity, it will be then that you will value this tiny spark of hope. This is the source of strength to be gracious, compassionate, forgiving, understanding, and reverent no matter what.

When this eternal spark moves you into graciousness, compassion, forgiveness, gratitude, kindness, understanding, and reverence, this becomes the foundation for sustainable happiness and success. When this happens, that is the miracle.

WHAT'S NEXT?

Dear friend. **If you have read this far you have read much.**
At this point you will have traveled a journey mostly in the
intellect. You have perhaps a renewed perspective of what spirituality means.

But I'm passionate in dearly wishing you to grasp and feel the
deeper joy and meaning of your life and existence here on Earth.
When you do so, you are aligning with your purpose and taking
spirituality to practical, everyday moments in life.

Whenever you think of spirituality no longer think of something that is mysterious or separate from your everyday activity.
Think of spirituality as the driver of your everyday activity whether
it be sleeping, eating, worrying, singing, dancing, driving, working,
crying, or being angry, sad, glad, or afraid. Think of it as a quest
to discover and understand your purpose for being—and then
becoming that purpose.

Whenever bad things seem to happen to good people, you may
ask why. You may ask "Why me?" From this point, you can choose
to be the "mystified" person who accepts that your life must be
ruled in mysterious ways by a magical and often not present God.

Or you can choose to be the "empowered mystic" who doesn't need to imagine and hope for a mysterious miracle, but instead engages in everyday life.

Consider what I have shared. Please do try the "crying meditation" more than once. It is a meditation that bridges healthy reality-based skepticism into spirituality. Please also practice the chakra rotations; they will help ease any body tightness or pain as well as deepen your knowing of the seven basic chakras. Keep doing both and you will deepen and come to know even more than what I have shared with you so far.

Consider what I've shared as a start towards scraping off more of that paint that covers up the window through which you see life. If and when you are ready in pursuing more, then you can follow up in the book *Spirituality for REAL: Deep Healing*.

No matter what you decide to do, you will come to find your own independent "source" of the truth of what is. You will come to find your own way...**the way**. In that way you will eventually come to meet your deep inner self of who you are...you will also come to find all others. ***We are all waiting for you, dear friend.***

You are not alone. You are loved. You are beautiful. I know it can be hard. You don't have to do anything if you don't want to. But at the very least still try to just keep showing up and be present. You need not be as scared...because you are never alone.

But even if you are scared and even if you still believe you are alone,

that is OK.

You are human. And have good reason to have developed the fears and beliefs you currently have.

And regardless of what you do or do not believe,

And regardless of what you have or have not done,

You are lovable because you were created.
You are loved because you exist.